10.00

D1708805

# Everything You Need to Know About Getting a Job

Working is a great way to earn an income and gain independence.

# Everything You Need to Know About

# Getting a Job

Carlienne A. Frisch

Rosen Publishing Group, Inc./New York

Published in 2000 by The Rosen Publishing Group, Inc.
29 East 21st Street, New York, NY 10010

Copyright © 2000 by The Rosen Publishing Group, Inc.

First Edition

**Library of Congress Cataloging-in-Publication Data**

Frisch, Carlienne, 1944–
    Everything you need to know about getting a job / by Carlienne Frisch.
        p. cm. — (The need to know library)
    Includes bibliographical references and index.
        Summary: Explains how to get a job, including information on everything from social security cards to resumes and networking tips.
    ISBN 0-8239-2961-2
        1. Vocational guidance—Juvenile literature. 2. Job hunting—Juvenile literature. [1. Job hunting. 2. Vocational guidance.] I. Title. II. Series.
HF5381.2 .F74 2000
650.14—dc21
                                                        99-047575
                                                          CIP

*Manufactured in the United States of America*

# Contents

# Introduction

These days, everything costs money. We pay for video rentals, tacos, hamburgers, and gas for our cars. In some fast-food places, we even have to pay for an extra plastic cup! Often teens need extra money for necessities—things that you really need, like food for your family or money to help pay rent. Or you may want a job to earn money for extra things like CDs or a car. A job will allow you to earn money for fun and for things that are very important. But looking for a job can be a confusing and frustrating experience if you are unsure of where or how to start looking. To find out what you already know about getting a job, ask yourself the following questions:

- What kind of tasks can I perform well?

- What kind of skills or talents do I have that I can put to use in a job?

- Where should I look for a job?

- How should I talk to a potential employer?

- What should I write in a cover letter?

- Am I even clear about what a cover letter is?

- What is a resume, and how do I write one?

- How can I find out about the company where I want to apply?

- What do I need to know about filling out a job application?

- What kind of questions will an employer ask in a job interview?

- What should I do after I have been interviewed?

- After I am hired, what can I do to be a successful employee?

If you do not know the answers to these questions, you probably feel nervous. But don't worry. Looking for a job is not difficult when you are prepared. Whether you want to work part-time or full-time, this book will help you find a job. In chapter one, you will find out how to look for a job that best suits your interests, your skills, and your education. Chapter two discusses how and where to look for work. You will learn about job advertisements, employment agencies, and networking—meeting people who can help you find the right job. In

Filling out applications correctly is an important job-hunting skill.

chapter three, you will learn how to contact employers, and you will see examples of phone conversations, cover letters, and resumes. You will learn how to fill out a job application in chapter four. Chapter five will prepare you for a successful job interview. The last two chapters will tell you about how to protect your rights on the job and how to be a successful employee.

# Chapter One | Preparing for Employment

**Y**ou may have decided that you want to look for a job. Well, the very first step is to apply for a Social Security card. The good news is that this is free! It is possible that your parents got your Social Security card for you when you were younger. However, if this is not the case, you can apply for one at your local Social Security Administration office. You will find the address and phone number of the office by looking in the phone book under U.S. Government. If you cannot find a Social Security Administration office in your area, call the national toll-free number at (800) 772-1213 and ask for assistance.

In order to fill out the application (a sample is shown on the next page), you will need to show proof of your age and U.S. citizenship. To prove your age,

# SOCIAL SECURITY ADMINISTRATION
## Application for a Social Security Card

Form Approved
OMB No. 0960-0066

| | | | | |
|---|---|---|---|---|
| **1** | **NAME** TO BE SHOWN ON CARD → | First *Shanesia* | Full Middle Name *Mae* | Last *Smith* |
| | **FULL NAME AT BIRTH** IF OTHER THAN ABOVE → | First *Shanesia* | Full Middle Name *Mae* | Last *Jefferson* |
| | **OTHER NAMES USED** → | | | |

**2** **MAILING ADDRESS** Do Not Abbreviate →
Street Address, Apt. No., PO Box, Rural Route No.
*2672 Avers Avenue – #4*
City *Chicago,* State *IL* Zip Code *60623*

**3** **CITIZENSHIP** (Check One) →
- [✓] U.S. Citizen
- [ ] Legal Alien Allowed To Work
- [ ] Legal Alien **Not Allowed** To Work
- [ ] Other (See Instructions On Page 1)

**4** **SEX** →
- [ ] Male
- [✓] Female

**5** **RACE/ETHNIC DESCRIPTION** (Check One Only—Voluntary) →
- [ ] Asian Asian-American or Pacific Islander
- [ ] Hispanic
- [✓] Black (Not Hispanic)
- [ ] North American Indian or Alaskan Native
- [ ] White (Not Hispanic)

**6** **DATE OF BIRTH** *06/05/86* Month, Day, Year

**7** **PLACE OF BIRTH** (Do Not Abbreviate)
City *Chicago,* State or Foreign Country *Illinois*
Office Use Only FCI

**8**
**A. MOTHER'S MAIDEN NAME** →
First *Marissa* | Full Middle Name *Annie* | Last Name At Her Birth *Jefferson*

**B. MOTHER'S SOCIAL SECURITY NUMBER** (Complete only if applying for a number for a child under age 18.) →
`3 2 5 - 5 5 - 5 5 5 5`

**9**
**A. FATHER'S NAME** →
First *Michael* | Full Middle Name *Jordan* | Last *Smith*

**B. FATHER'S SOCIAL SECURITY NUMBER** (Complete only if applying for a number for a child under age 18.) →
`5 5 3 - 3 3 - 3 3 3 3`

**10** Has the applicant or anyone acting on his/her behalf ever filed for or received a Social Security number card before?
- [ ] Yes (If "yes", answer questions 11-13.)
- [ ] No (If "no", go on to question 14.)
- [✓] Don't Know (If "don't know", go on to question 14.)

**11** Enter the Social Security number previously assigned to the person listed in item 1. →
` __ __ __ - __ __ - __ __ __ __ `

**12** Enter the name shown on the most recent Social Security card issued for the person listed in item 1. →
First | Middle | Last

**13** Enter any different date of birth if used on an earlier application for a card. →
Month, Day, Year

**14** **TODAY'S DATE** *04/05/2000* Month, Day, Year

**15** **DAYTIME PHONE NUMBER** *(312) 555-0000* Area Code / Number

DELIBERATELY FURNISHING (OR CAUSING TO BE FURNISHED) FALSE INFORMATION ON THIS APPLICATION IS A CRIME PUNISHABLE BY FINE OR IMPRISONMENT, OR BOTH.

**16** **YOUR SIGNATURE** *Shanesia Mae Smith*

**17** **YOUR RELATIONSHIP TO THE PERSON IN ITEM 1 IS:**
- [✓] Self
- [ ] Natural or Adoptive Parent
- [ ] Legal Guardian
- [ ] Other (Specify)

DO NOT WRITE BELOW THIS LINE (FOR SSA USE ONLY)

| NPN | | | DOC | NTI | CAN | | ITV |
|---|---|---|---|---|---|---|---|
| PBC | EVI | EVA | EVC | PRA | NWR | DNR | UNIT |

EVIDENCE SUBMITTED

SIGNATURE AND TITLE OF EMPLOYEE(S) REVIEWING EVIDENCE AND/OR CONDUCTING INTERVIEW

DATE

DCL

DATE

Form **SS-5**

You will need a Social Security number to work legally in the United States.

you will need either your birth certificate or one of the following: a hospital record of your birth made before you were age five, a religious record made before you were three months old, or your passport.

If you are a U.S. citizen (whether born in or outside of the country) and have a U.S. passport, you can show this document to prove both your age and your citizenship. But if you are not a U.S. citizen, you need to show proof of permission to work in the United States. This proof would be a current document issued to you by the U.S. Immigration and Naturalization Service (INS), such as Form I-551, I-94, I-688B, or I-766. You will also need another proof of identification that shows you are who you say you are. You may use any of the following documents:

- Driver's license

- Passport

- Adoption record

- School identification card

- Insurance policy

- Another official form

A Social Security number is essential for any legal work in the United States, so make sure you know what your number is and keep your card in a safe place.

## Knowing Your Rights

Until you reach a certain age, usually sixteen, your state's laws may prevent you from getting a regular job. The laws were made to protect children from being forced to work. But don't worry, occasional jobs such as baby-sitting, mowing lawns, and taking care of people's pets are not affected by these laws.

Once you reach the legal age of employment in your state, an employer cannot refuse to hire you because of your race, your gender (whether you are male or female), your national origin, your religion, or a handicap that is not related to your ability to do the job. An employer cannot use any of those reasons to pay you less than another new employee with the same job. These are your rights. An employer who breaks any of these laws is guilty of discrimination and should be reported to the federal or state labor department. Some states have additional laws to protect workers. Ask for more information at a WorkForce Center or Job Service office.

## What Kind of Job Do You Want?

*Lisa, fifteen, is outgoing and especially enjoys being around children. Lisa is frequently asked to baby-sit, and many of "her" kids tell Lisa that she is their favorite! She has taken child development courses in high school and has really enjoyed them.*

12

*"I want to look for a full-time job at a child care center after I graduate from high school," she says. "I'll get as much experience working with children as I can, and I'll save up for college. After that, I hope to become a kindergarten teacher."*

*Lisa's job choice fits well with her outgoing personality, her skills, and her past experience with children.*

*Believe it or not, Miguel, seventeen, would rather spend time with a computer than with his friends.*

*"I work at the hardware store after school," says Miguel, "and even though my job is to stock shelves, the store manager asks for my advice whenever a computer doesn't work properly. My dad wants me to become a partner in the family landscaping business, but I know I want a career in the computer industry."*

*Next summer, Miguel plans to get a job as a repair person in a computer store.*

If you aren't as certain as Miguel and Lisa are about what kind of job you want, don't panic. You can talk with your school guidance counselor about the classes you have enjoyed the most, or ask him or her to give you educational achievement tests. These tests will show where your strong points and weak points are in math, writing, reading, spelling, and grammar. You

Baby-sitting is excellent preparation for a career in child care.

can also ask to take aptitude tests, which measure your natural abilities, such as your hand and eye coordination, mechanical ability, memory, reasoning, and your communication skills. There are also tests that can assess your interests.

## Figure Out Your Likes and Dislikes

If you are not clear about what you think you would prefer doing as a job, try making a list. Under two separate headings—Likes and Dislikes—list what skills you enjoy and what things you are not so fond of. You could also try the following quiz to figure out your preferences. With each of the following questions, choose the answer that best describes you. Then look for a pattern in your answers.

1) I enjoy working with . . .
    a) ideas
    b) people
    c) things
    d) my hands

2) I like . . .
    a) newness and change
    b) to talk with people
    c) to get things done right
    d) making things

3) I would rather . . .
    a) spend the afternoon talking with a
       foreign exchange student
    b) plan a party for Saturday evening
    c) spend my evening on the Internet
    d) devote the weekend to fixing my car

If you chose "a" for most of your answers, you may be best suited to a job that offers action, change, and challenge. You might look for a job that will allow you to do a variety of work. You would probably not enjoy a job where you do the same exact thing every day.

If the majority of your answers were "b," you may want to look for a job that provides a lot of contact with people, like teaching, sales, customer service, or counseling. If you chose "c" for your answers, you probably have an eye for detail and would like to work in a quiet

Use your school or public library to research different types of occupations.

environment. For you, bookkeeping would be a better choice than sales. If you chose "d" for the majority of your answers, you might enjoy working as a mechanic, carpenter, or plumber. Jobs in sales or bookkeeping are probably not right for you.

## Make Use of Your Library

You can find books in your school or public library that give detailed information about many kinds of jobs. The following in particular are very helpful:

- The *Occupational Outlook Handbook* describes hundreds of jobs currently available in the United States.

- The *Dictionary of Occupational Titles* provides job descriptions for thousands of jobs.

- *VGM's Careers Encyclopedia* gives information on nearly 200 jobs, including a detailed description of each job—outlining working conditions, what qualifications and education are needed, starting and average income, potential for advancement, and additional sources of information.

When you are able to narrow down the list of what particular types of jobs interest you, you can further refine your search at the library. If you need assistance locating a certain book or are not sure how to go about searching the stacks, ask the librarians for help.

# Chapter Two

# Looking for a Job

**N**ow that you know what kind of job you would like, you can start looking for one. The following are suggestions of where you can look for a job:

- Your school's counseling office

- A bulletin board at your community center, church, or even at a supermarket

- The classified advertising section of your local newspaper

- Your state's WorkForce Center or Job Service office

- Private employment agencies

- The Internet

- Leads from friends or family members

Check the classifieds every week for job leads.

# Newspaper Advertisements

In the classified section of the newspaper, look under the heading Employment or Jobs. You should be aware, however, that the way newspaper listings are presented may vary depending on the size and organization method of each newspaper. In larger newspapers, different jobs in the same field may be listed under various subheadings. For example, if you are interested in the field of health care, you could look under the following headings or subheadings: Clerical, Sales, Education, Medical, in addition to Health Care. Jobs may also be listed in alphabetical order.

Here is an example of three classified ads for the same kind of job. They are listed in alphabetical order. The first ad appears near the top of the health care job listings section, the next ad was placed in the middle, and the third ad was at the end.

In between these listings will be other health care openings. If you are looking for a job as a nurse's aide, you will miss the first and third ads if you look under only Nurse's Aide in the listings.

Arbor Villa, a 40-bed facility in Santee, CA, is hiring nurses' aides. Apply with a letter of interest to Linda Gomez, Director, Arbor Villa, 1425 Camino del Rey, Santee, CA 92071

Health Care
**Nurses' Aides**
Nurses' Aides for assisted-living facility in small southern California community.

Send resume to
Ron Schweim
Hillside Manor
P.O. Box 555-C
La Mesa, CA 92041

Work in a new health-care facility. Hiring RNs, LPNs and Nurses' Aides. Call 800-555-5555, ext. 26, for application information.

You will see some larger ads on the same page of the newspaper. These are called display ads. They also list employment opportunities. They seldom are in a particular order, so be sure to look at each display ad to see if it interests you.

# WorkForce Center

You can get free information about jobs at the local WorkForce Center office. In some states, the WorkForce Center is called the Job Service office. Your parents may refer to it as the Unemployment Office. Even though the name has changed several times, the purpose is the same—to help people get jobs. Look under Employment in the government section of your local phone book for the address of the nearest WorkForce Center or Job Service office.

At the WorkForce Center, you will have access to a computerized database of employers who are looking to hire employees. Using a computer to search for jobs, you will type in information—your interests, skills, salary requirements, and work schedule preferences—and the database will provide you with a list of jobs that will be tailored to your preferences and skills. The list will include information on how to contact the employers.

### The Job Training Partnership Act

At the WorkForce Center, you can also learn about resume writing classes, job search workshops, the Job

Training Partnership Act (JTPA), and the Job Corps.

JTPA provides services for low-income people, those who receive public assistance or whose families receive it, and high school dropouts. The services include career counseling, funding for training, and assistance with child care and transportation for up to two years of training time. The Job Corps offers assistance in education, training, and employment to high school dropouts who have been in trouble with the law.

## Private Employment Agencies

Private employment agencies provide employers with employees. Some agencies specialize in certain kinds of work, such as office or computer jobs, construction and skilled trade jobs, or in-home cleaning or health care jobs. In some states, private employment agencies may charge a registration fee. But many states have passed laws that prevent agencies from asking a person who is looking for a job to pay a fee.

If you register with a private employment agency, you will have to sign a contract. Make sure you read and understand every part of the contract. If you have questions about it, do not sign it until you have asked someone you trust to read it and to help you understand it. Under the terms of one kind of contract, the agency will find a job for you with an employer who has listed the job opening with the agency. You will become an employee of the company for which you work. The

Many employment opportunities are posted on the Internet.

agency will receive a percentage of your wages or salary for a certain period of time.

Under a different contract arrangement, you will become an employee of the agency. The agency will pay your wages. You will be assigned to work for a company that also has a contract with the agency, but you will not be an employee of that company. If you want to work part-time, only on certain days of the week or only during certain times of the year, you would benefit from this kind of arrangement. If you want to work regularly all year, you may be sent to work at one company. When your contract with the agency is about to expire, you may want to apply for a job with the company instead of renewing your contract with the agency. Or you may decide to continue as an employee of the agency.

When you apply for work with a private employment agency, you can expect to be tested for skills, aptitudes, and interests. You will also be interviewed by a job counselor who will find work that suits you. You should be completely open and honest with the counselor. The agency may provide you with insurance benefits and specialized training. Training on certain computer systems is common. You may have to pay a fee for the training, so you should learn as much as you can about working on computers while you are in high school.

## The Internet

There are many Internet sites that list job openings. If you do not have access to the Internet at home, ask a librarian at your school library or at the nearest public library to help you begin your job search on the Internet. There are many employment Web sites and search engines. You can begin with JobBank USA MetaSEARCH. The Internet address is *http://www.jobbankusa.com*. There you will find many search engines for job vacancies. If you want to learn more about searching for a job on the Internet, ask your librarian for the most recent edition of the book *Job-Hunting on the Internet*. If your library does not have it, ask to borrow it through interlibrary loan.

## Networking

Networking is another way to get a job. You can ask family members and other adults with whom you are

Your school may have an employment office or board.

acquainted if they know of any job openings. You can also ask them for help in getting a job that you know about. If your neighbor's brother owns a Pizza Hut that employs students after school, you might ask your neighbor to put in a good word with his brother before you apply for a job there.

*"I work weekends at a fast-food restaurant, but I want a full-time office job after I graduate from high school," says Shanesia. "So I began checking the job listings at the school counseling office. None of them interested me."*

*"I told my mom," she continued, "and she said that I should look in the newspaper."*

*Shanesia looked and saw three full-time jobs*

*that suited her—administrative assistant, office assistant, and secretary. She called the phone number listed for each ad and learned that the employers hoped to fill the positions within two weeks, too soon for Shanesia to apply now.*

*Shanesia then visited the WorkForce Center in Fargo, North Dakota. The instructions on the computer were easy to follow. She filled out the form and then told the computer to search for and print out job listings that fit her application.*

*"I got a printout for seven job openings later on!" Shanesia exclaimed happily. "I am sure that by the time I graduate, I'll have a great full-time job that I like."*

# Chapter Three

# Contacting Employers

**W**hen you get in touch with a potential employer (someone for whom you would like to work), try to make a good impression on him or her. It is important to be honest. Do not pretend to have education or experience that you do not have. Your goal is to have the employer want to hire you. You can make a good impression on a potential employer via phone calls, your cover letter, and your resume.

## Phone Calls

When you phone a company about a job opening, you may speak with a secretary, a human resources director, or with the person in charge of the department or office that has the job opening. In a small company, you may even speak with the company owner. Whomever

27

Be fully prepared before calling about potential jobs.

you speak with, try to make a good first impression. You will impress people if you speak clearly, are pleasant and confident, and are organized in terms of knowing what you want to say.

Have the ad or computer printout about the job in front of you, along with a pen and paper. Make your phone call from a quiet place. If your home is too noisy, ask your school counselor if you can make the call from school. Try not to talk too fast or sound nervous.

Practice what you want to say. For example: "My name is Dylan Wolfe. I'm calling about the maintenance mechanic's position you advertised in the newspaper. I am interested in finding out more information about the job. Can you please give me the name of the contact person to whom I should send my resume?" Be sure to ask for the correct spelling of the person's name and for the company's full name and address.

If you reach an answering machine or voice mail when you call, listen carefully for the instructions and push the correct buttons on the phone so that you can leave a message. Your message can contain the short speech you have already prepared, plus the following: "You may reach me at my home phone, (777) 555-5555, any day between 3 and 5 PM. I look forward to hearing from you."

If you do not hear from the employer within two days, you can call again. Being politely persistent may give you an advantage over other applicants.

## Your Cover Letter

Some job ads will ask you to send a resume—a type-written page that outlines your work and education experience, and describes any special skills you may have. (Resumes are discussed later in the chapter.) Be sure to include a cover letter, which goes on top of, or "covers," the resume. Your cover letter should have the following:

- A short introduction that includes:

    a) The reason why you are writing the letter. Example: "I am writing to inquire about the maintenance mechanic's position you advertised in the newspaper."

b) An explanation of why you are interested in the job. Make your letter sound
original and personal, but not phony.
Example: "I became interested in engines
when I was ten years old and have planned
a career in mechanics ever since. The job
you advertised sounds like a good match
with my experience and interests."

◆ A paragraph that indicates your skills and/or
experience. Explain what skills or experience
you have that would make you an ideal person
for the job. Example: "I have taken all of the auto
mechanics, engine maintenance and repair,
welding, and related shop classes offered at my
high school. I earned an A grade in most of
them and a B in the rest. For several summers, I
have worked with my uncle, who owns Wolfe's
Auto Repair in Washington, Pennyslvania."

◆ A description of what you would like to have
happen. Example: "I would appreciate the
opportunity to speak with you in person. I've
enclosed my resume and hope to hear from
you soon."

◆ A phone number where you can be reached.

◆ A signature at the end of the letter and your
mailing address.

Always have someone else proofread your cover letters.

Read your letter out loud to hear if it sounds both businesslike and not too stiff. Proofread the letter several times, checking over your spelling and grammar. If you are using a computer, use the spell-check option. It will catch spelling errors but not some typographical errors (typos), such as writing "from" when you meant "form." You should ask someone else to look for typos and grammatical errors in your letter. You might ask a teacher to help you make sure that the letter is correct.

Use a business format for writing your letter. This is a particular style of letter writing that is considered the most professional. To see an example of the business format, look at the sample cover letter on the next page.

May 10, 2000

Mr. Jordan Harris
Harris Auto Repair
9898 Commercial Road
Pittsburgh, PA 15222


Dear Mr. Harris:

I'm writing to inquire about the maintenance mechanic's position you advertised in the newspaper. I became interested in engines when I was ten years old and have planned a career in mechanics ever since. The job you advertised sounds like a good match for my experience and interests.

I have taken all of the auto mechanics, engine maintenance and repair, welding, and related shop classes offered by my high school. I earned an A grade in most of them and a B in the rest. For the past three summers, I have worked with my uncle, who owns Wolfe's Auto Repair in Washington, Pennsylvania. He says that he is pleased that his nephew has a real knack for making cars run well.

I would appreciate the opportunity to speak with you in person. I've enclosed my resume and hope to hear from you soon. You may reach me at (777) 555-5555 any day between 3 and 5 PM, and all day Saturday.

Sincerely,

Dylan Wolfe

Dylan Wolfe
26320 S. Spring Street
Pittsburgh, PA 15222

# Writing the Right Resume

Your resume is your advertisement to a potential employer. It is a written statement of your job qualifications, including your education and experience. Your resume, which includes some of the facts mentioned in your cover letter, will give more detailed and specific information about your skills, abilities, experiences, and career interests. A resume also includes your name, address, and telephone number. You do not need to give your age or use a photo on your resume.

The first section of a resume should describe your career objective or interests. For example, Angela Rojas wrote: "My career goal is to own and manage a women's clothing store. I enjoy making people look and feel good in the clothing they wear. I am currently seeking work in women's clothing retail."

Then you should list your experience (if you have any) and your education. In order to clarify for yourself how much and what kinds of experience you have had, make a list. Look at each item and pick the ones that best show your skills and experience. Angela wrote: "Since junior high school, I have sewn most of my own clothing and have made clothing for several of my friends, including one prom dress. From this, I learned which fabrics and styles flatter different body types."

When you list your education, you should include the name of the school you attended or graduated from, the year you graduated, and the location of the school. You can also list specific classes that have helped you prepare for a particular job. Angela made sure her resume mentioned the course in sales and marketing that she took.

Many people write "References available upon request" as the last section of their resume. Employers know they can ask for references. Instead, add information that will make you stand out. Angela wrote: "I was active in Distributive Education Clubs of America (DECA) in high school and took part in several successful sales projects."

There are many ways to prepare and design a resume so that it is appealing to the eye. You may want to use books like *Resume Magic*, by Susan Britton Whitcomb, or *Resumes for Dummies*, by Joyce Lain Kennedy, for ideas on how to make your resume look good. When you check out a book about resume writing from a library, be sure to get a book that has been written in the past few years. Resume styles change, so it is not a good idea to use an outdated book.

Your resume should be professionally typed on good quality paper. If you cannot do this yourself on a computer, you should get someone to do it for you. Do not use erasable typing paper. If you can afford it, have your resume prepared at a printing business. Look in the phone book or Yellow Pages under the heading Printing to find a business in your area.

# Chapter Four

# Applying for a Job

**W**hen you apply for a job, you will probably be asked to fill out an application form. Even though most or all of the information asked for is already in your resume, you should fill out the whole application neatly and clearly. Those in charge of hiring know exactly where to look for each person's education, skills, and references. A completed application form makes it easy for the interviewer to do his or her job.

When you go to a potential employer, you should take several things with you. These include your Social Security number, a copy of your birth certificate, an identification card with your photo, and two copies of your resume. You may need to give one copy to someone at the company, but you should keep the other copy so that you can easily transfer information from your

When seeking references, pick people who know you well.

resume to the application form. Bring along a list of three references—people who know you well and can attest to your skills and character.

Choosing the right people as references is important. Though you can sometimes use a relative who doesn't live with you as a reference, most of the time you will be asked to list other people who know you well, such as a teacher. Other suggestions are a neighbor who knows you well; a person for whom you baby-sit or do small jobs; or someone from your church, synagogue, or temple. Before you list a person as a reference, contact the person for permission. Ask the person if he or she will feel comfortable telling the employer that you are honest and dependable. If the person hesitates, do not list him or her as a reference.

## Your Appearance

Wear clean, neat clothes when you apply for a job. Dress as if you are ready to go to work *that* day. Wear business clothing when applying for an office job. If you apply for a mechanic's job, wear clean work clothes, such as jeans that are not torn and a work shirt. Make sure your hands, nails, face, and hair are neat and clean.

After you fill out the application, you may be asked to come back another day for an interview. Or you might be interviewed as soon as you have filled out the application.

## Learning About the Company

If you apply for a job at a local store or business where a friend or relative works, you may already have information about the employer. If not, try to get more information about the company at your local public library or on the Internet. You can learn if the company made a profit in the past several years and how the profit compares to profits in similar companies. This information will help you decide if your job will be secure after you are hired. Try to familiarize yourself with the products and services the company sells. This will help you ask questions during the interview that show you are interested in the company. You will also be able to tell the employer why you are the ideal person for the job.

Always look neat and professional for job interviews.

*Before Angela applied for a job at Fabulous Fashions, she went to the public library to look at the store's advertisements in the local newspaper. She also asked the librarian for information about the store's history. Angela learned that the store's owner, Roxanne Johnson, had been in business for twenty-five years. In the newspaper, Angela saw that the store advertised a sale as a "fashion fling for full-figured women." When she visited the store, she saw that the clothes were in sizes fourteen to twenty-six. Now Angela had a better idea of what she would say once she got a job interview.*

# Chapter Five

# Interviewing for a Job

**W**hen an employer calls you for an interview, it means your application or resume illustrates that you are qualified for the job. The interview is your chance to stand out from other applicants. The three important parts of a successful interview process are preparation, the actual interview itself, and the follow-up.

## How to Prepare for an Interview

In chapter four, you learned how to get information about the company. This information can help you make a list of reasons why you should get the job you want. List the skills and personality traits that make you the best choice for the job. Then rehearse for the interview. Practice telling the interviewer about your skills and personality traits. Try several ways of answering interview questions. You will learn which answers sound the most natural. You will also become more confident and more relaxed.

These are some of the questions you may be asked in an interview:

- *"Tell me about yourself."* Tell the interviewer how your past related experience (if any) makes you the ideal choice for the job.

- *"What are your strengths?"* Talk about your skills and positive personality traits.

- *"What are your weaknesses?"* Answer with a trait that you are working on improving. Explain how you are doing that.

- *"What was your favorite subject in school?"* Tell why you preferred a particular subject.

- *"What are your short-term goals?"* You can talk about your plans for employment and for further education (if you plan to go on in school).

- *"What do you want to be doing five or ten years from now?"* Make sure your answer is realistic.

## Practice Interviewing

*Angela practiced for her job interview in front of a mirror. She checked for good posture and eye contact. She pretended to be the interviewer and said, "Tell me a little about yourself." Then Angela took the part of the job applicant. She knew that Fabulous Fashions specialized in clothing for larger women, so she knew what to tell the interviewer. Angela looked in the mirror, smiled, and answered. "As my resume shows, I have been sewing clothes for myself and for several friends since junior high school. I know what fabrics and styles compliment larger people. One of my best friends is very heavy, and she always tells me that the clothes I sew for her make her feel good about how she looks."*

*Angela smiled again. "I also help my aunt, who is a large woman, pick out the clothes she buys. And you can see that I'm not a thin person. I can relate to your customers. I love to help people feel good about how they look. I think I'm the perfect person for this job."*

*After rehearsing for the interview, Angela knew she could give solid reasons why Roxanne Johnson should hire her.*

You also should make a list of questions you may want to ask the interviewer. Write them down so you can show that you are prepared. The list will help you remember to get all of the information you want about the particular job you are applying for. You may want to include the following questions:

- ◆ What are the major responsibilities of this job each day? Each week?

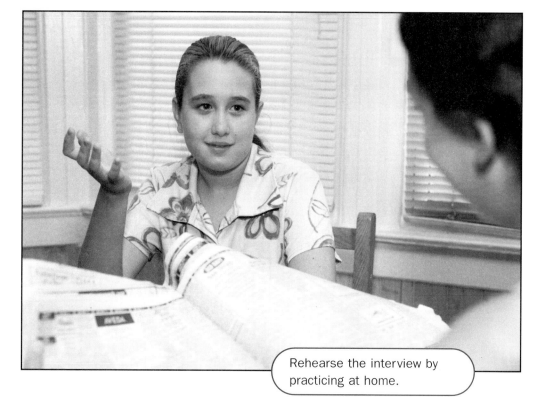

Rehearse the interview by practicing at home.

- Will I be trained in a planned program or as the need for learning occurs?

- How long did the last person who had this job work here?

- Why is this position open? Is it a new position?

- Can you tell me about the company's future plans?

- If I am hired, to whom will I report?

- What is the wage or salary range for this position?

There are several more questions you may want to ask. You may ask these questions if you are called for a second interview or when you are offered the job. Here is a list of additional questions:

- What are the policies on sick leave, vacation leave, and flextime?

- Where would I work? May I look around?

- What are the opportunities for travel?

## The Interview Itself

Dress appropriately for the interview, as you learned in chapter four. Confirm your interview appointment the day before. Plan to arrive for the interview about ten minutes early. If you must be late, call ahead and explain why. Even with a good excuse, you will start off with one strike against you. Be courteous to everyone. If there is a receptionist, introduce yourself. You can say something such as, "Hello, I'm Angela Rojas. I'm here for a one o'clock job interview with Ms. Johnson."

You may be told to have a seat in a waiting room until the interviewer comes for you. When the interviewer arrives, stand and introduce yourself again, offering your right hand for a handshake. Your handshake should be firm, not limp. The interviewer will lead you to a private room. Do not sit down until your interviewer asks you to do so.

Give the interviewer your full attention. Maintain eye contact, but don't stare. Try to relax and be yourself.

Always give a firm handshake when introduced to employers.

Remind yourself that you rehearsed for the interview and you know what you are going to say. Listen carefully and think before you give an answer. Don't interrupt the interviewer. Use the interviewer's name when answering or asking questions. If you have had a job before, do not say anything negative about your previous employer or coworkers.

At the end of the interview, thank the interviewer for the opportunity to discuss the job. Repeat one or two key reasons why you are a good choice for the job. Ask when you should contact the company again. If you want the job, say that you are interested.

*At the end of Angela's interview with Roxanne Johnson, Angela said, "Thank you for talking with me about this sales position with Fabulous Fashions. I'm sure my experience sewing and choosing clothes for larger women can be put to good use at your store. May I call you next week? I really hope you will give me the opportunity to work for you."*

## The Follow-Up

When the interview is over, you should stay in contact with the employer. Write a personal note within two days, thanking the interviewer again for giving you the opportunity to meet her or him. Include a brief list of the skills and personality traits that make you a good choice for the job. Say that you are interested in the company and in the job. Mention a specific date when you will call the interviewer. Be sure to call on that day to ask if you are still being considered for the position. Being politely persistent may be what it takes to get you the job you want.

# Chapter Six

# If You Have a Disability

If you have a disability—a physical or mental impairment—your right to work is protected by the Americans with Disabilities Act (ADA). An employer cannot use your disability as a reason not to hire you if you have the skills and abilities needed to do a certain job. However, the ADA cannot guarantee that you will find a job.

Perhaps you feel that your disability will keep you from getting a job even though an employer is willing to hire you. If that is how you feel, you may need to develop more self-esteem. Take some time and think about the things you have done well.

About three-fourths of the top industries in the United States hire people who have disabilities. Small companies also hire people with disabilities. Many people with disabilities hold manufacturing jobs. There are also many job opportunities in companies that specialize in technology. The number of technology-related jobs is growing steadily. And many people with disabilities are able to use computers and other technology just as well as those without disabilities.

A job can bring you many rewards. Here is a list of some of them:

- Feeling good about yourself for doing a job well

- Helping others

- Learning something new

- Testing your limits

- Meeting new people

- Getting a regular paycheck

Before you begin looking for a job, you should consider your interests and skills. You may want to reread chapter one. Then, you should learn how to look for a job (outlined in chapter two) and how to contact potential employers, which is discussed in chapter three. You must learn how to apply for a job (chapter four) and interview for a job (chapter five), just like people who do not have a disability. Decide what special skills you can offer an employer. Then be prepared to explain them to her or him.

Employment enables adults with disabilities to live successfully on their own.

## What You Can Do Now

Your teachers and your school counselor can help you decide on a job and a career. Ask your counselor about aptitude tests. Ask for help in making a work-study arrangement. It will give you work experience while you are still in school. You can also gain experience by doing unpaid work as a volunteer. Your counselor may have a list of volunteer opportunities that you can choose from.

What must you do to compete for a job with a person who does not have a disability? The *Vocational Assessment and Curriculum Guide* lists eleven general skills you should have for entry-level jobs:

- You should be able to solve basic arithmetic problems.

- You should be able to tell and follow time in hours and minutes.

- You should be able to go to work an average of five times per week.

- You must understand the importance of going to work every day and arriving on time.

- You must be able to move safely within the job environment.

- You must understand how to behave appropriately on the job.

- You should be able to read instructions that consist of at least one or two words.

- You should be able to do repetitive tasks for at least thirty minutes.

- You should be able to learn a new task if you are given six to twelve hours of instruction for it.

- You should be able to work for at least three hours without stopping.

- You should have the desire to work for money.

You should not limit yourself to entry-level jobs because you have a disability. You may be eligible for specialized training for higher-level work. The *HEATH*

*National Resource Directory on Post Secondary Education and Disability* lists work and education resources for people with disabilities. Ask a librarian to help you check out a recent edition.

You may believe that an employer has discriminated against you because you have a disability. The U.S. Equal Employment Opportunity Commission (EEOC) can help you. You can contact the EEOC at 1801 L Street NW, Washington, DC 20507, or phone (202) 663-4900. The EEOC Web site is *http://www.eeoc.gov.*

# Chapter Seven

# After You Are Hired

If you are hired, your employer may require you to take a test to show that you are drug-free. Your employer will pay for the test.

You may have an orientation session your first day on the job. During the orientation, you will learn more about the company and about what your boss expects from you. You will learn when and how often you will be paid. You will be asked to fill out a W-4 form. It is a tax form on which you will indicate how many family members you are supporting. You may claim yourself on this form. The amount of tax deducted from your paycheck will depend on what you write on the W-4 form.

If the company has a time clock, you will be given a time card that you will use to "punch in" when you get to work and "punch out" when you leave. You will be told if you can take your lunch break and other breaks whenever you want to or if all employees take a break at the same time. You may get a tour of the business. If your job requires you to wear a uniform, your employer will provide uniforms for you.

It is important for you—the new person—to get to work on time every day, even if other employees arrive late. You should be prepared to begin work as soon as you arrive. You should stay until the end of your shift every day.

## Work Culture

After you begin work, you will learn how to do your job. You will also learn about the company's "work culture." This includes how people dress and the way they relate to one another on the job. The work culture includes the goals and values of the business. You may also hear a "work jargon." These are words used only by people who work in a certain job. Restaurant workers have a jargon that is different from the language spoken by health care workers. Mechanics and models each have their own job-specific vocabulary, too. You will have to learn the specific terms and expressions that may be a part of your job, but don't worry—it's exciting to learn new words!

Be pleasant to everyone at work, even if someone is unpleasant toward you. It will help you make friends and will make everyone's work easier. No one wants to work with a grouchy person. After a while, you will probably have a favorite friend or buddy at work. This person can help you understand the work culture. You can also learn more about the work culture from the company newsletter (if there is one) and from other printed materials about the company.

Do not be afraid to ask your supervisor or boss any questions you may have. You are not expected to know everything about the job or the company. One question you should ask is whether the company has casual Fridays. This is the day when many businesses allow employees to "dress down." They do not dress as formally as they do the rest of the week.

Some businesses have a booklet that helps new employees learn about the company. The booklet may include maps of the building. It might include forms and procedures for getting things. You may need to use a form to get such things as a computer log-on identifier or office supplies. There may also be a list of whom to contact for problems, such as a burnt-out lightbulb.

Do not bring your personal problems to work. If you have an argument with someone in your family just before you leave for work, do not show your anger to the people you work with.

Do not use the phone to make personal calls except in an emergency. You have been hired to work, not to chat with friends. Tell your friends not to visit you at work or to call you there.

Talk to your supervisor about any questions or concerns.

After you have some experience in your job, you may want to get a better job with the same company. Ask your supervisor for advice on how to do this. It is against the law for anyone at work to ask you for sexual favors as payment for helping you to get a better job or to keep your job. A person who asks you that is a criminal. If this happens to you, tell the person "no." Then report the crime to the EEOC. Your state also may have an office where you can report the crime. The law protects you from losing your job because you reported the crime.

If you do your job as well as you can and pay attention to the work culture, you will be well on your way to success in your new job.

# Glossary

**applicant**  Person who is seeking or applying for a job.

**cover letter**  Letter of application for a job, accompanied by a resume.

**employee**  Person who is paid for working for another person, business, or organization.

**employer**  Person, business, or organization that hires and pays other people to work.

**employment**  Work, occupation, or business.

**employment agency**  Business or organization whose purpose is to bring together a job seeker and a prospective employer.

**full-time**  Usually thirty-five to forty hours per week, or a full workday, usually seven to eight hours.

**interview**  Meeting between an employer and an applicant for a job, either face-to-face or on the phone.

**network**  Arrangement of connections.

**networking**  Developing and using connections, such as friends and acquaintances, for help in getting a job, advancing in a job, or accomplishing other things.

**part-time**  Work period less than a full workday or full workweek.

**resume**  Written statement of your job qualifications, including education and experience.

# Where to Go for Help

## In the United States

Center for Economic Options
601 Delaware Avenue
Charleston, WV 25302
(304) 345-1298

Contact national organization for local address. The organization works to provide access to job training and employment options for women.

Equal Employment Opportunity Commission (EEOC)
1801 L Street NW
Washington, DC 20507
(202) 663-4900

Helps persons who believe that an employer has discriminated against them.

Jobs for America's Graduates (JAG)
1729 King Street, Suite 200
Alexandria, VA 22314
(703) 684-9479
e-mail: ars@imd-net.com
Web site: http://www.jag.org

Contact national organization for local address. Has programs for disadvantaged and at-risk students who have limited work experience and do not plan to attend college immediately after graduation or are at risk of dropping out of high school.

SER—Jobs for Progress National
100 Decker Drive, Suite 200
Irving, TX 75062
(800) 427-2306
e-mail: hguajardo@sernational.org
Web site: http://www.sernational.org

SER, or Service, Employment, and Redevelopment, provides employment opportunities and training for Spanish-speaking and disadvantaged Americans. Contact national office for local address.

Vocational Industrial Clubs of America (VICA)
P.O. Box 3000
Leesburg, VA 20177-0300
(703) 777-8810

VICA tries to interest young people in trades and in

technical, industrial, and health service careers; develops students' leadership abilities and sense of civic responsibility. There are VICA clubs in most states.

WAVE
501 School Street SW, Suite 600
Washington, DC 20024
(800) 274-2005

Helps disadvantaged sixteen- to twenty-one-year-old high school dropouts and students at risk of dropping out find unsubsidized jobs.

Wildcat Service Corporation (WSC)
161 Hudson Street
New York, NY 10013
(212) 219-9700

Provides transitional employment and training for former substance abusers, economically disadvantaged mothers, out-of-school youth, illiterate and delinquent youth, and former offenders.

# In Canada

Human Resources Development Telecenter
(416) 730-1211
Web site: http://www.hrdc-drhc.gc.ca

Provides information on applying for Social Insurance Number (the Canadian equivalent to the Social Security Number.)

# For Further Reading

Baratz, Lewis R. *VGM's Guide to Temporary Employment.* Lincolnwood, IL: NTC Publishing Group, 1995.

Bolles, Richard Nelson. *Job-Hunting on the Internet.* Berkeley, CA: Ten Speed Press, 1997.

Clemens, Lynda and Andrea Dolph. *How to Hit the Ground Running in Your New Job.* Lincolnwood, IL: NTC Publishing Group, 1995.

Editors of VGM Career Horizons. *VGM's Careers Encyclopedia.* 4th ed. Lincolnwood, IL: NTC Publishing Group, 1997.

Hirsch, Arlene S. *Interviewing.* New York: John Wiley & Sons, 1994.

Kennedy, Joyce Lain. *Resumes for Dummies.* Foster City, CA: IDG Books Worldwide, 1996.

Kissane, Sharon F. *Career Success for People with Physical Disabilities.* Lincolnwood, IL: NTC Publishing Group, 1997.

Lamplugh, Rick. *Job Search That Works: A Proven 10 Step Program.* Menlo Park, CA: Crisp Publications, 1991.

Marler, Patty, and Jan Bailey Mattia. *Networking Made Easy.* Lincolnwood, IL: NTC Publishing Group, 1998.

Mendenhall, Karen. *Making the Most of the Temporary Employment Market.* Cincinnati, OH: F&W Publications, 1993.

Paradis, Adrian. *Opportunities in Part-Time and Summer Jobs.* Lincolnwood, IL: NTC Publishing Group, 1998.

Pesmen, Sandra. *Dr. Job's Complete Career Guide.* Lincolnwood, IL: NTC Publishing Group, 1996.

Raye-Johnson, Venda. *Effective Networking: Proven Techniques for Career Success.* Menlo Park, CA: Crisp Publications, 1990.

Webb, Susan L. *Step Forward: Sexual Harassment in the Workplace.* New York: MasterMedia Ltd., 1991.

Whitcomb, Susan Britton. *Resume Magic: Trade Secrets of a Professional Resume Writer.* Indianapolis, IN: JIST Works, 1999.

# Index

# Index

## About the Author

Carlienne Frisch is a freelance writer of books for children and teens, as well as career profiles and business and travel articles. Her nonfiction children's books have covered such topics as franchising, pet care, advertising, map reading, European countries, substance abuse, and author Maude Hart Lovelace. Frisch is a mass communications instructor at Minnesota State University in Mankato, Minnesota.

## Photo Credits

Cover by Brian T. Silak. P. 38 by Simca Israelian; p. 45 by Shalhevet Moshe; p. 49 © Greenlar/The Image Works; all other photos by Brian T. Silak.

## Design and Layout

Annie O'Donnell